TAKE

SHOWCASING EXCITING NEW POETS
EDITED BY ANNABEL COOK

spotlight poets

First published in Great Britain in 2007 by
Spotlight Poets
Remus House
Coltsfoot Drive
Peterborough
PE2 9JX
Telephone: 01733 898101
Fax: 01733 313524
Website: www.forwardpress.co.uk
Email: spotlightpoets@forwardpress.co.uk

SB ISBN 1-84077-162-3

Foreword

As a nation of poetry writers and lovers, many of us
are still surprisingly reluctant to go out and actually
buy the books we cherish so much. Often when
searching out the work of newer and less known
authors it becomes a near impossible mission to track
down the sort of books you require. In an effort to
break away from the endless clutter of seemingly
unrelated poems from authors we know nothing or
little about; Spotlight Poets has opened up a
doorway to something quite special.

Take A Look is a collection of poems to be cherished
forever; featuring the work of ten captivating poets
each with a selection of their very best work. Placing
that alongside their own personal profile gives
a complete feel for the way each author works,
allowing for a clearer idea of the true feelings
and reasoning behind the poems.

The poems and poets have been chosen and presented
in a complementary anthology that offers a variety
of ideals and ideas, capable of moving the heart,
mind and soul of the reader.

Annabel Cook
Editor

Contents

THE POETS & THEIR
FEATURED COLLECTIONS

JEANNIE ANDERSON

I was born in Derry City, Northern Ireland, in 1964. I have five sisters and two brothers younger than me.

I have been writing for years, firstly as therapy to a trauma I went through, as a way of healing. I started to write poetry when I joined Galliagh Women's Group as an administrator. I was doing courses in drama with a great local playwright called Irene McLaugh; I told her of my writing and she put me in contact with a writers' group that was bringing work from both sides of our communities together. We published a book called 'Decades' and I was thrilled to have three pieces of my work entered.

My children are my inspiration in some of my writing, also my partner, Kevin, who realised the full potential in me and pushed me forward. My own life experiences are brought strongly to my writing; love, lust, loss and some hard-hitting poetry. I'm currently writing children's stories and wish to have them, and my poems, published in books that I can call my own.

I attend a weekly writers' group here in Derry City called 'The Playhouse Writers'. They are great support for writers of all types. They're a great bunch of people and you're always sure of a laugh, as well as their support in your endeavours to being published by running courses from creative writing to playwriting. At the end, all this is put on in a showcase of work done.

I find that my poems just flow onto paper like they were always meant to be there and I carry a book and pencil everywhere. At present I am setting up my own business.

Inside Of Me

In the middle of my own love story
Sparks within me
I'm alive
Blood's pumping, tears flow
Body quivers
Loss upon my face
Adrenaline rushing
Endorphins threading through my body
Bearing down
Deep breathing
Body wants to hold on
Heart-stopping contractions
From my inner sanctum
Relaxing
Head lightening, gas 'n' air
Life's pain goes on and on
Release less frequent
Sweat pooling in my body's dips and crevices
Gibberish chatter
This, the new life
Presents herself in my love story
My infant
Welcome to my world.

Playful Fairies

Look over there
Can you see
The fairies and their pals?
Ladybirds, dragonflies and bumblebees
Playfully flying up and around
Hiding in daisies and bluebells

The woodland is barely lit
By the sun's rays
Stretching, pushing its life
Through the trees
Somersaulting fairies

Wehey, look at them go
Tig in mid-air's an amazing sight
The fairies dart left to right
Wings of satin
Catching the light

Singing and calling
Trapezing off a few blades of grass
Oops!
They've seen me
They're gone in a flash

Empty Nest Syndrome

I'm an abandoned mum
Feeling unused, unneeded, unloved
I understand you've to make your impression in the world
Please don't forget about me
The maturity of life
Has taken you from me
I no longer, alone, can protect thee
Where once I was home, love, security, life
Everything you needed to blossom
Remnants of you lying on the bedroom floor
Your room half-empty of you
Your presence gone
Is this what 'empty nest syndrome' feels like?
No more innocent daughterly hugs and kisses or pranks
Your world is yours
I'm not allowed in, am I an embarrassment
When I show you my affection?
I'm not sorry for that
I'm only sorry that you have grown up

Orgasmic Arch

Gut-wrenching belly-flipping emotions
Deep groin notions of motion
Moisture looms from the inner soul
Erotic fantasies of us together
Breathing and heart-pulsed orgasm
Drawing body and mind
Lubricated by love's nectar and odour
Mind-penetrating orgasmic lightning
Thunderous movements, passion crashing
Two bodies prickled
Like butterflies darting at our bodies
Body hair standing on end
Pleasure sure to explode again
Arching back in orgasmic seizures
Grinding thrusts out of body
Satisfied fluid lacking
Sweat salts converging along our bodies' seams and creases
Mortality rears waves of mini emotional tornadoes
As the body and mind land
Crumpled into the other's torso
No longer of this mortal existence
Souls return from le petit mort
Our little death
The little death

Innocence

Clouds shaped like boats
Way up in the sky
A plane, a cow
Can cows fly?
Can elephants be pink?
Of course they can
The innocence in you
Can make anything be
The word itself
I have no sense
Explains anything you can see for yourself

SP, DD, Kaelie, Kevinna
Whose little minds growing up were and always
Will be my inspiration.

Love Burns

True love does burn your emotional soul
Scarring it deeply
Only one person
Allows the scars to grow
As your love and lives develop
Dependence on the other
Becoming suffocating
Not existing without the other
Be the guardian of your soul
As the clouds are the shoulders of the world
And you become that one person
Who controls
The scars of your emotional soul

The Full Storm

Turn around
Look at me
Lustful leers across to you
Read my thoughts
Look inside of me
Tell me what you see
It's you I want
You are my need
Passion
Buzzing head to toe
Kiss me deep, meaningful and slow
Sending tsunamis to engulf my brain
Touch me
Release the full storm
From deep within me to my groin
Make love to me
Caress my form
Release my soul
Wanting, pleasing, emotionally strong
Heighten my senses, all not one
Ear-piercing sensitivity
Deafening breaths
I want your lips to melt into my body
Released from this world
As our bodies shudder
Euphoric blush reveals itself
Our storm is a secret no more

The Angel

Clouds gracefully drifting by
So light
As the angel that learnt to fly
Wings of love, warmth and security
Let us all please feel your purity
Shine your grace upon us all
Rays of wonderment
Surround your form
Warding off incoming storms
Featherly dancing from cloud to cloud
Flowing behind you
A draught-rippled shroud
The angelic music seems all around
Your feet barely touching the clouds
As you leap
I wish I were you
Not just in my sleep
Dancing sunrays crowning your trailing locks
With an awe-inspiring halo
Magnificent beauty, the smile on your face
Gazing at me, drawing my stare
I glance away to a nearby cloud
That engulfs you
On passing you are gone
Knowing in my heart you're with me right now

Paradise

You craving your paradise
Receptive to your amorous advances
Begging inwardly
Wanting to give it all away
Wanting more
Closing in
Allowing you to lift me up
Carrying me away to your land of pleasure, and lust
Passionate kisses fall onto melting lips
French kisses, between watering mouths
I am, giving myself to you
Knowing
I will not come to any harm
Gripping my seams, you gently position my body
To receive you
Gently sending my body into orgasmic cravings
For more pleasure
Breasts firmly pressed to your chest
Uncontrollable desires called in voice
As both fluids mingle
Rushing blood, senseless whispers
Of love
We allow the pulsed pleasure shocks
To burn themselves out
One mind
One machine
Paradise

For Evermore

As we grow old together
I love you even more
Our youthful bodies
Now giving into time
The breasts that fed our children
Dried up and firm no more
Bones once agile
Now creaking and sore
Our eyes still
Along with our hearts
And love
Youthful for evermore

Our Journey

Looking ahead
No turning back
For our journey is only to be forward
Our family indeed has travelled a distance
To be here right now
Excursions, crossroads and junctions barely
Remembered
Decisions made
Right or wrong
Are like the world's own vascular system
All roads leading to a new vision
At times it gets clogged
And it takes the skill of the traffic surgeons
Removing the clot in the bitumen lifeline
To continue our journey
To our future

Love's Blush

Love's blush
Captures my body
As I drift to Earth
I don't wish to land
Eyes only for you
Caressing each other's bodies

Brushing your manly chest
Drawing out your form
With my fingertips
Firmly gripping
Your strong thighs
The perfect specimen of manhood

You are breathtakingly beautiful
To my being
Our bodies feel as though
They are meant to be
As one
As we wrap together

Becoming one
Mind
Heart
Body
As love's blush
Begins to fade

Releasing me
Body
Mind
And spirit
Back
To the real world

Your Wings

Enter into my life
Sweet angel
Bless me with
Your generosity
To forgive
To move on
To forget
I know you're here
I feel you near me
Sending shivers down my spine
As you wrap me up in your wings
Hold me
For a little while
I need that love
Show me what you see
Help me step into my future
Sure and secure I'm doing right

BERYL DOBSON

Beryl Dobson, born in South Yorkshire, is a housewife, now retired from a life in a wide variety of careers from tax officer to wages clerk to costing and purchasing clerk. She has three children and six grandchildren.

Her hobbies include sewing, reading, gardening and listening to music, both live and recorded. In her younger days she loved sports, and in 1997 she ran the London Marathon for the 'Heart Foundation' raising £1,360 in sponsorship.

Give Me Something

Give me something to remember
When I'm old and grey
Give me something to remember
To my dying day.

Give me something to remember
When the skies are no longer bright
Give me something to cling to
Far into the night

Give me something to cherish
And remember for all time
Give me something precious
That I can call, all mine

Give me something special
That I can look back, and say,
All I asked of you, dear
Was true love, every day!

I Lie Awake

I lie awake
The whole night through
I lie awake because
I'm thinking of you

Sleep doesn't come
Because I'm missing you
Perhaps it will
With the morning dew

Oh-hum! I'm feeling blue
Why do I keep thinking of you?
You're just a record, on my brain
As it turns . . .
It drives me insane.

Nowhere

There's nowhere in the world
That I would rather be
There's no one in the world
Than you - for me

For no matter where I go
My heart tells me, I know
That there's nothing left
For me to discover

For this love
That I hold dear
I couldn't find
In many a year

And as the seasons
Drift by
I'll cherish it -
Till I die.

Take The Chance

If ever, there was a time,
. . . It's *now*
Not yesterday, or tomorrow
. . . But *today!*

Because the chance,
May never come
Your way again.

So get on
With the task ahead
Seemingly difficult . . .
Perhaps

But with fortitude
And inner struggles, overcome,
An adversity . . .
Can be turned into
A success, take a chance.

My Heart Won't Forget

I may forget the date,
The hour or the week.
I may forget a message
Or even, forget to speak.

I might forget, a person,
A name, or street or home.
But I know, I'll never forget
You, no matter where I roam.

For I can forget important things
And minor ones too,
But my heart
Won't *ever* let me,
- Forget *you!*

The Longest Memory

Love has the longest memory
It never forgets
Whether it's night or day
It passes the test.

It can be days, weeks
Months or *years*
Love will shine through
Laughter or tears.

Love is the teacher
Love is the reaper
Love is the master
It can conquer *all* . . .

Love will be the reminder
Of deeds, words and thoughts
Long forgotten . . .
Lying sleeping, and dormant
Waiting for love, to awaken . . . love.

Reflections

I wish I had time to tell you
All you mean to me,
But my thoughts
Must stay hidden forever
So the world cannot see.

Sometime, perhaps
I'll let you have a glimpse
Of what I really feel.
Till then, my heart stays
Locked and barred
And I alone, have the key.

If it's only for a moment
If only for a day,
To meet and to hold you
This is what I pray.

So let us have some happy memories
To store away for the coming years,
For some thoughts will fade forever
But those of you, my love,
I know, will never!

For like the mirrors of reflections
My soul is laid bare
And yet no one can see or know
What is hidden *there*.

Give Me

Give me, a love
Full of promises
Some, perhaps - not kept
- And yet
A love, that
Stirs the heart
So it never forgets.

And give me a love
So far-reaching,
Not in denial
But measured mile by mile
Shore to shore,
And even more.

So that, this is
The beginning
- And not, the end
Of all our hopes
And schemes
And all of
Our wishes, and dreams.

Don't Forget

Don't forget to remember me
For you can forget any number
Or the day or time too

You can forget to laugh or sing
But darling, just remember
I love you

You can forget to
Post a letter
Or catch a bus on time

You can forget, all the answers
Or the poem,
That doesn't rhyme.

But darling,
Don't forget to -
Remember *me*.

Life's Footprints

Making footprints in life
Making your mark
In the waking sunlight hours
Or by the moonlight's rays
- At eventide.

For as you journey through
The passage of time
Such a lot to achieve
You have to believe
And hope the journey - is smooth.

So that the decisions
- You make
The route, that you take
Is right . . .
For *your* sake.

Don't look back, and say
'If only -
I had done that
Or gone, another way.'

Have faith, that you
Are on the right path
As you surmount
Obstacles that come your way.

For when you come
To journey's end
You can look back
- And say,
'Nice to have known you -
- My friend.'

Just Believe

I'll be by your side
When you *need* me
I'll be by your side
When you *call*

For no matter what it takes
I'll be there . . .
Somehow, somewhere
So that moment
You will recall.

For the past
Will never be, forgotten
It will never be, erased.

For the memories, of you
Will linger
And your sweet
And loving face.

Take Me

Take me *through* . . .
The dark shadows
Into the sunlight.

Take me *from* . . .
The doom and gloom
To a future,
Sunny and bright.

Take me *to* . . .
A brighter tomorrow
With laughter -
Not tears.

Take me to *wherever*
Your dreams are.
To make them - mine *too*
Banishing all my fears.

Sorrow

Aah! Sorrow that lies within
Stirs the heart, remembering
So lonely, and yet
Never will I forget.

Sorrow, the master
The taskmaster, the ploy.
Don't disguise the truth
And hide the joy.

Sorrow, with never good intent
Steals in, is never sent.
In sorrow, thoughts lie
Sometimes in disguise
. . . I wonder why.

I Once Knew A Guy

I once knew a guy
Who said he was free
I once knew a guy
Who said he'd make me happy!

I once knew a guy
Who said, he'd *never* roam
But he never hung his boots up
- In my home.

For he was a roamer
Yes, a roamer
Roaming here and there
Far and near.

So you see I never knew
When he'd appear
Although I waited
Year after year.

But although, he was a roamer
The ties, I couldn't break
For in my heart - he nestled
Asleep and awake.

If I Could . . .

If I could undo
All the wrongs
I've done to *you*
I *would*, dear

And *if* I could
Put right
This very night
By turning back the clock
- To yesterday
I *would*, dear

And *if* I could take back
Those hurtful words
And put *others* in their place
You *know*, I would, dear

Then *maybe*
Just *maybe*
There'll be a chance
For me, with you, again

For things could be
Oh, so different!
And we wouldn't be
Saying goodbye again.

ELIZABETH CHEVERTON

She was born in Kenilworth. Her father's family have lived in the small triangle bounded by Barston, Berkswell and Kenilworth, for almost four hundred years. This is probably why her poetry has a recurrent theme of connection with the earth for, as she says, 'All my grandmothers are part of the Warwickshire soil.'

Her great love of the country comes from her childhood, when she and her father would go walking in the fields around Kenilworth. 'He could always find something interesting and unusual, white violets, yellowhammers' nests in gorse bushes, blackberries or mushrooms, depending on the season.'

She was educated locally at King's High School for Girls, Warwick, and apart from staying at home to look after her children for twelve years, she spent her working life at various branches of Barclays Bank. Her interests are in gardening, cooking, music and reading.

Her favourite poet is Edward Thomas, who was killed in the First World War. 'I very often find lines in his work that describe my feelings exactly, in the same phrases that I would like to explain them.'
Her passion at the moment is growing vegetables on her allotment and, at times, many weeds - bindweed, fat hen and dandelions! But she is an optimist and hopes that the cold winter will always help her beat the invaders, ready to plant the beans, courgettes and tomatoes next year, in what she thinks of as 'magic dust'.

She has written poetry since she was a child, especially at times of emotional upheaval. Her poetry is on the subject of relationships as a woman with her family, the outside world of friends, and with the countryside.

It is with reference to her roles as daughter, wife, mother and lover, and the struggle to be something quite apart from a 'relationship' - a figure in the landscape. She says, 'As a non-believer in a life after death, I wanted my afterlife to be something more than, as they always say in the obituaries, 'loving wife, mother and grandmother'.

She is living happily in Leamington with her third husband, Malcolm.

Significant Feelings

Somewhere along dark corridors of past,
Significant times are remembered,

Like stations on the Underground;
Meetings, partings.

Winds blow in that deep Tube,
Warm from one station, cool from the next,

Smelling, long after the platform has disappeared,
Of the air of significant feelings.

Yearnings to be loved -
To love is all too easy,

The sick fears of a dark night,
Aching for the touch of the land,

Pain that never produces a scream,
Hilarity that never laughs aloud,

Everyone's Siamese twin,
Significant feelings.

AM

The world was left outside, last night,
And has grown a mouldy green frost,
Like a slice of forgotten bread.
The children dance with warm white feet,
Gas heating, eating toast, then gone,
Some eager, resigned, and one sad,
Leaving under a warm pillow
The red-spotted jewel of a tooth,
Misplaced and fairy-forgotten.
In the washing machine window
Everyone's last week revolving.
The four-foot-high bearded baker
In brown-paper-bag-coloured coat,
Drags out his four-four-six basket,
Eagerly dripping with doughnuts.
In the queer, quiet time passing
Canary Cordelia sings,
Sun shines the grass green as parsley.

Sonnet To The Sister

Feather-fondling the boy with her delight
In his promise of being different
Pleasuring in him, young and innocent,
She flicks his tolerant cheek, lips all tight.
A loving gesture, this, as from her height
Of six more years, apparently all spent,
Becoming woman, caring shoulders bent,
She gazes on his little body white.
At frosty dawn he comes, pillow-dragging,
His innocence erect, as he seeks her love
And she pulls him onto her gentle breast.
Old and guilty, these memories nagging,
Could they be strangers, like vulture and dove,
Returning from each rare meeting distressed?

The Hamlet

July moon daisies in the mowing grass,
Are they young hares that cause the flowers to sway?
Among the crumbling crosses, yellow-mossed,
The vicar's wife and lover threshing, lay.
From orchard - hidden lines, that summer night,
Had slipped a will-o'-the-wisp, but quicker,
He gathered silk and lace, black, pink and white,
The village girls left, without a knicker.
Along the lane, dry on the summer leaves,
Hung Fred Lee's clothes, while he in frock-coat sat,
Playing on his flute for the performers,
Holding teeth to tail, dancing rat to rat.
To the church with rod, the vicar started,
And in the font, the sticklebacks darted.

Brown Roses

One day, she thought he loved her
That windy litter-lifting noon
Among the brown roses.

The wind tugged her over the hill
Down to where he was waiting.
Pushing the truant hair from her brow,
She saw the warming in his grey eyes.
He kept her talking,
Did she wish to go?
Shyness made words,
His voice weakened her again.
Drunk with the things she loved,
Pale face, pale eyes,
She thought that they loved her,
That she saw fire.
How could they light it
When they had so many innocents to burn?
This year's dead flowers
And letters saying little but his name,
She has them there.

One day she thought he loved her,
That windy litter-lifting day,
Among the brown roses.

Joining

Over and ever, breaking, joining, from the beginning,
History choosing the severing and we the grafting.

Sometime, black, in a workshop welding
By a goggle-faced priest
A 'sparkler' wedding of brittle parts,
Unmoving, rusting.
Maybe a twisting of ribbon and hair,
Tightly restricting,
The shining river, brown bee velvet
Crushed in the plaiting.
Over and ever, joining, breaking,
Sewing, transplanting,
Tender tissue sometime rejecting,
Broken hand-stitching.
Fat hen - free deep in a gardener's den,
Purposeful, planting,
Two stems curling, rose and clematis,
Catalogue mating.
But wild in the ditches, 'old man's beard'
Spirals entangling,
Covers the ripening elderberry,
Joining and seeding.

Over and ever, joining, combining, wind-chance arranging
History choosing the severing, but we, the grafting.

The Song Of The Somerset Lad

I was free as a bird, other stories I'd heard,
And vowed that I'd never encumber
My young carefree life, with a thing called a wife,
Till I went to a dance in Stogumber.

I'd done 'Strip the willow' with a girl like a pillow
And then the band played a rumba
And swirling her kirtle, came a redhead called Myrtle
And altered my night at Stogumber.

She made my thighs tingle, why want to be single?
I squeezed her, I gave her my number.
I said, 'I'm just simple.' She said with a dimple
'All the boys are like that in Stogumber.'

Seven weeks - we were wed, we bought a new bed,
Though on it we rarely do slumber,
For she dances at night, with her red hair so bright,
Just for me, on my knee, in Stogumber.

The Death Of Nora's Husband

Misty days and dying wisteria,
Long June mornings of new roses and rain,
This early hour, the grey road, glinting glass,
Like silver, winnowed from ripening corn.

Two multicoloured caterpillars of cars, still,
Watching the measuring, the fence flattened,
The empty bus, not seeing the driver
Weeping white, the cycle's twisted pattern.

Women and men, the early office talk
Of the day's search, before they know a name,
From an anxious face, facing a clean fork.

She types all day, the draughtsmen stand and joke,
They rattle the silver for tomorrow's flowers,
When she'll sit on her own and weep and choke.

Tutti Frutti

Oh! If my voice were like a lark,
I'd sing my love a ballad,
In the heavy summer nights,
I'd feed him on fruit salad.
Oh, that my lips were berries,
My eyes, two big black grapes,
I'd frown and smile, to make my love
Wine, when we embrace.
I wish that I were soft,
With skin like peaches' bloom,
I'd tempt my love to take a bite
While lying in his room.
If pomegranates were my breasts
And my love wished to eat,
I'd offer not two gooseberries,
But something smooth and sweet.
And if we lay in orchards
In daisies, love and hay
I'd offer him Eve's apple
Throughout the drowsy day.

Cutting The Cord

By a buttercup slope
Winds the dark water.
It's a rope
Of your shining hair, lovely daughter.
If only my body were freer, I would run
To the edge to the deep,
To the sedges, to be numb,
Like the touch of your frozen voice as I weep.

Once so near, you and I,
On the day that we parted,
Wet dark head against thigh, did we cry?
We did, but not broken-hearted.
When it was all begun,
Remembering,
I loved you more born than unborn,
After our severing.

Come, Friendly Bottle

Come, friendly bottle, you can hide in me,
And I in you. We can hold each other
While the nightmares drift over
And we become leg-loose.

You can fill this empty room with smiles
Without having to smile back,
Warmth with no bills,
Happy forgetfulness

Of fragile years, handled with care,
Smashed bones and a perfect mind's eye
Full of sun and past springs.

Bacchus, when we become estranged,
The green buds are locked,
Everyone laughs, and I watch.

Dance For A Double-Decker Bus

It all began with the pears.
Seeing them from my window,
Gold in the grey October,
As the sun rose.
Making the leaves Christmas-green,
Baubled glass, hanging heavy,
Bright breasts of a warm woman,
In the sunshine.
Then with a harp and the beat,
I began to drift, I danced
Round the room of books and flowers
In the sunlight.
Touching the fans as I passed,
The lace, the pink velvet chair,
My arms were chiffon-graceful,
With sun inside.
Humming, dancing and smiling,
I looked again - the window,
A tall bus, waiting, ticking,
Full of faces.
Dreaming with milky music
Happy in the morning light,
I sang, hung, golden, glowing,
Like a ripe pear.

Friday Night

'Friday night is music night'. We begin
Four movements of the Symphony of Glass,
Loud on the ears of pavements, sharp on skin,
Moving you to tears, slicing us who pass.

Friday night, third-hand February snow,
Lies on the wharf, by sun-neglected wall.
Battle drums boom, untrained, unarmed we go,
No trenches dug where walls of windows fall.

Flat pictures on the screen might make you talk
For half an hour, of rage and blighted lives,
But fear is my companion as I walk,
My neighbours' pockets warming guns and knives.

Friday night was music night, us kissing,
Where's the fun when half my face is missing?

Playing The Organ At Old Milverton

I don't believe I could die for a cause,
Just refusing the 'skilly', to change laws.
You would be lost, if God had decided
To give His only begotten daughter
Me, to be crucified, to save the world
I don't believe I could die for you all.

Once I was part of the edge of a fight,
The hypocritical lunge to the right,
One of the front row watching round the ring.
Now I'm moving away, just listening
To the playground games of wild Westminster
Waiting for the bell to ring - and 'order'.

For the pleasure of touching keys and stops,
Oh! I'll play the music, not say the words.
I can't hear the voices, I smell the grass
Lying in hot heaps outside the dark church,
Hear the bird hovering and singing high
Above the meadow where I want to be.

A Good Harvest

Will I have a good harvest
Ripe-red with fruit, golden leaf,
Before the winter that comes to us all,
Black bare branches, with no hope of spring?
Will my arms be full
Of the apples of friends and family,
Hips and haws of a happy life,
Or will an early frost, an autumn gale strip me clean?
Can I imagine among my twigs
A silver nutmeg, a golden pear,
Someone so special that my little nut tree
Will shine throughout this coming winter?
What makes a good harvest?
A gentle budding, a warm spring.
Did I have a warm spring?
The temperature was not high!
But I had a hot summer,
Sometimes too hot, almost tropical.
I had a later flowering,
Feeling like a full-blown poppy.
But will I have a good harvest,
An Indian summer of late heat?
Can I store the fruits of my life,
Eating apple pie into my old age?

ALASDAIR SCLATER

I was born in South Africa into a family of teachers and managers. I grew up with the South African plains all about me, and the reality of Apartheid all around me. Twelve years ago my dream was realised and South Africa became a democracy. It was the greatest day of my life!

I came to London to escape Apartheid reality and have lived here for the past twenty years. For me London is a love/hate relationship. I miss the space and nature of my South African home but in London I can connect to every culture of the world.

I studied zoology in search of a conservation career. I came to Britain when quite young and have lived all my adult life here. For most of my life I have worked in the horticultural field being alternately a gardener and a teacher of the subject at a further educational college.

Poetry is a field I have discovered quite late in life. Poetry for me is a way of exploring my feelings and the different strands of my identity that span two countries and two cultures. It allows me to express different perspectives of the world as I see it.

My recurrent interests are wildlife and nature and they form a large part of the inspiration of my poetry. In addition, I am influenced by my interest in history and in different cultures. Another great influence is that of my Christian faith. Some years ago I converted to the Orthodox Church and as a practising Christian, the themes of Christian belief also have an influence.

A Whale For A City

Why is one of the defining moments
When a city all of a sudden has a whale for company?
When one member of the species wanders up the river
To see all of the life in a city of this multitude
Where life seems condensed into a marvellous glitter of people
and cars

There the whale is surfacing in the middle of the Thames
And the crowds applaud and cheer
At the sight of this monster of the deep
Everywhere there is the news of how the whale arrived to join
the throng
And swim in the vicinity of the Albert Bridge
Where from did it arrive
This deep sea denizen of the North Atlantic?

Why did it leave its place
In the deeps to arrive in the depths of the ordinary world
Of the hustle and bustle of a city
Obsessed with making money
To provide entertainment for the multitude that knows no other?

Yet arrive it did to take over the news
For a few days we have heard of little else
Maybe it got confused with sonar soundings in other places
And went where it should not go
The heavenly salt of the deep
Replaced by the freshwater of the upper reaches
Of a river where nothing else awaits
But the freshwater that will rush into every wound
Expanding it from nothingness to something great
Its skin not adapted to this new world of freshwater

Yet all the while humans await
And worry and fret over the state of it
Modern technology is brought to the fore to save the whale
And there it is carried on the boat
Down the river
Draped in a tarpaulin
People putting water over it
While an attempt is made to look after it
And keep it safe
For all the world to marvel at
Carried in a barge down the Thames
Hopefully to find rest in the cool Atlantic
And they line the river
The people watch it pass
All muttering a silent prayer
'Let it live!'

. . .

Yet how sad is the news that now we hear
The next day
That at seven o'clock
Or thereabouts
The whale dies
With all the city
Retiring to mourn
The sadness
Of the bad ending to
An otherwise wonderful saga.

An Unusual Vista

How many times have I walked the street
That leads from Lambeth
Down to Elephant
Knowing full well that street
Yet one day
I suddenly saw a vision of a Mediterranean
Sunshine
With a pergola covered in ivy
All the poles were covered in lush growth
Beckoning to
A vista beyond
That spoke of lush garden secrets
Hidden from normal eyes

It was worth a stop
To look
Closely at this place
That seemed to transport
Immediately to distant lands
Lands of summer sun and warmth
With the old white building elegance

There it was, the view framed
In a little garden that I had never noticed before
On closer look
There were a few plants
And some desultory swings
And other paraphernalia
Of a children's playground
Along with this pergola
Not quite so splendid on closer inspection
Rather neglected in fact
Behind there was a council estate
Yet how was it, just a bit of neglected planting
At the right time can transport
To lands of distant sun.
Forgetting the well-known street outside?

Nature Confined

Is it possible to feel the pain
Of the great forces of nature confined
As the rivers are confined and constricted
Beneath our feet
Forced to flow in pipelines underground
Away from the skies above
Nature's forces
Constricted in the vessels of our tunnels
Where nothing else remains
But the vanity of Man
Overpowering the dark forces beneath
And force them below ground
Unseen
To wend their constricted way

Where do we see the power of the earth
Sunk forever beneath our feet
The power of wind bounded by what we do
How we shut out the elemental forces

Staying in the times that we show
Bounded in times of nature's might
Not to change the lives
Of those of us who are here

The Banks Of The Thames

At low tide new land appears
So much to see
So little that can be seen
Yet there is a world in existence here.
That nobody sees in their workaday lives
How flocks of seagulls swirl around
Waiting for the next meal
And starlings and crows descend on the beaches.

There to troop in noisy assemblages
Looking for the denizens beneath the rocks
Here lies the meal of tiny crustaceans
That wait to be disturbed
On which they will emerge skipping and jumping
Almost too fast for the starlings in hot pursuit
Innumerable ones of them there are
Yet they bide their time in secret hideaways.

Till they are recovered by ravenous starlings and crows
Looking for an easy meal
Here they jump about amid the flotsam and jetsam
Bits of seaweed
With the shells of crabs
Sometimes with a ready meal inside
Or a small fish.
Among the myriad bits of life that somehow survive in this place
And provide food for the flocks of birds
Along this stretch of water
London's greatest river.

Thames Beach

At the edge of the concrete skyline
Caught at the side of the river
Within the concrete bounds
Sits the beach
At low tide it appears
The new land full of caked mud
Everywhere

Yet here is concealed the accretions of London civilisation
Two thousand years of it
Silently waiting in the river
For the fortuitous day
When it will appear from the grey ooze
Rising amid the sand brought from further afield
Yet this river, the artery of London
Conceals many treasures here

Maybe there appears something special
A Roman coin
Or a piece of old stoneware from Victorian times
Or the old metal objects from a medieval working
Or even better, old bones from prehistory
Debris of times gone before
All worked in amid the cups and plastic bottles of our modern era
Flotsam and jetsam
Of our modern throwaway society
That outnumbers
All the rubbish of generations gone before
How much of this can we find?
All litter somehow finds its way into the Thames
A truism of modern life.

Yet this mixes with that of the civilisations before
In a varied picture of our time and place.
That provides entertainment for modern Londoners
Finding sense in this old metaphor of our city

The Birds At Dawn

Dawn is breaking
And across the lake
The troups are grazing on the grass
Here stand the ranks of Canada geese
Giving just a little deference
To the human walker entering their domain

Around them the greylags are joining in the fray
Grazing on the grassy banks
It is easy now
With so few humans about in the grey February dawn
Cold and grey as it is

As I approach
There is a plop in the water
And the moorhens
Dart swiftly into the cold water
Swimming away from the banks
Hordes of coot depart as well
Continuing their territorial squabbles
As one or other becomes
Out of territory
And ready to be chased
By all and sundry others
How they fight each other splashing in the water
Chasing each other off their territories
In this cold dawn

The cormorant
Is doing an early bit of fish catching
Though this morning
There are no fishermen to anger
To cause to fulminate against
These birds
That take all their fish
So the cormorants have an easy run on the lake

Still the lake sits
Silent, transparent
Immovable
Under the cold dark sky

Mice On The Underground

How we relieve the tedium of a long journey
Waiting for trains
That always seem to take ages to come
Waiting at the sides
And viewing the miles of track
That snake beneath London's streets
All the dark brown of that line
We can see while standing on the platform
Yet here we are standing in this morass

Yet the bit of interest that is provided
Is the vision of the mice
That scamper around the tracks
Everybody is watching
The little furry beasts
Going about their business
At a safe distance from our houses
Where their reception would be somewhat different

Yet here
They run between the tracks
Sometimes emerging
To scamper
Along the platform
And all of the commuters
Are watching
The house mouse
One of our notorious pests
Running about their business
On the Underground

The Memory Of Crows

The grey overcast sky of an early April dawn
Gives a message of a new day to come
Where the ploughed-up lawns
Near a sports-turf
That is being developed
Cast a message of desolation in the early hours
There is something more to come in this place
Whether good or bad, nobody knows
Ahead and over the lamp posts
Come the cries and the harsh calls of the crows

At once above
At the side and around
The ghostly hours ring out as they do all over
Calling to each other
Their black forms
Bringing out few contrasts in the grey scene
Why this commotion in a scene where few travellers venture?

Is it a memory
Of food previously dispensed?
Where flocks congregate to see and take the latest scraps from the table
And leftover uneaten food from a throwaway society
Food on the turn
For birds with stomachs hardened by their carrion diet
That are stronger than anything we can take

Is it the memory of a stranger who once fed them?
Or is it the possibility of what they can take?
Or is it an idea
That here could spell some random food there
Given to them
To which they have become accustomed?
Maybe it is impossible to say
As the cries ring out in the grey dawn

DUGALD MCINTOSH THOMPSON

I am a young-at-heart 70-year-old, the first southern-born child to a north country family schooled in Bedford. My first job was as a trainee carpenter. When my national service was due, I joined the Royal Navy, Fleet Air Arm section, served three years, then left the Royal Navy in 1956. That was the first time I wrote any kind of poetry or verse.

To write poetry, I need to get inspiration and the content from world affairs, usually events that either make me angry, happy or sad.

Over the years I have lost count of the number of poems I have destroyed, usually because they are out of fashion or badly written and probably mean little to anyone else that might read them. The ones I keep, I consider to be worthy of reading.

I used to write my views to various newspapers but mostly it seemed a waste of time. Unless you are somebody very important, they do not seem to take much notice so I started, in earnest, to write my feelings in verse, hoping that some day, someone would take notice.

After I left the Royal Navy, I tried various jobs, opened a couple of shops, tried driving and delivery, managed a bowling alley, became a director of a company building vehicle interiors and then, for the last twenty-five years of my working life, I became self-employed, designing and building vehicle interiors. A great number of the vehicles I worked on were for major motoring manufacturers, also owner-operators, many of whom used to show their vehicles at shows around the country, often winning prizes, not only in the UK, but also in Scandinavian countries as well. I found this work very satisfying, giving me a livelihood that I loved as much as I love writing poetry.

People-Friendly

Black and white, white and black
Mixes well on the furry cat
The baby born that has no sight
Will grow to know black as night
And love and cherish every act
'Be people-friendly'
The power of the media is used with spite
It helps to add up to people's fright
In God we trust, we trust in God
So why do all religions fight?
Why can't they cherish a friendly pact?
'Be people-friendly'
The leaders of the world love greed
A dream of owning every seed
The seeds then grow to angry scenes
They want to kill and own the world
What stupid foolish people
'Be people-friendly'
Race, hate and anger come with ease
If only that energy was used to please
In this I say to all, remember
To every single burning ember
From birth to bone, everything is on loan
'Be people-friendly'

Human Shame

Rhino horn, aphrodisiac, elephant tusks,
Musk deer pods, Japanese whale meat.
China's tuna, dolphin nets,
Basking shark fin to Far East dins,
Forests gone, pandas lost, seal cubs clubbed,
Their parents slaughtered, cosmetic cruelty,
GM food, battery hens, beagles legless,
Monkeys smoking, swans and lead, fish float dead,
Slaughterhouse cruelty, aircraft pollution,
Not just cars to pollute Planet Mars,
Crops sprayed poison, insects gone, birds lay dying,
Foxes shot, mutant children, crippling drugs,
Their only saviour, a mother's hugs,
Horses, greyhounds drugged for money,
Puppy farms, crossbred felines,
Over-bred show dog, close-caged lions,
This for greed and human vanity
And every government backs this insanity.

England

England was so green and true
Memories were so very few
Unto England came a war
Memories then a little more

The death of our beloved King
Was more than just a passing thing
In fifty-two our lovely Queen
When work was plenty and poverty had been

Freedom created such a mess
When the sixties changed our common dress
The black and brown and the yellow
All tried hard to be the common fellow

The seventies same with a less adore
When everybody wanted more
The work was fading with a crash
And in crept the discriminative mass

Swept in the eighties, policies changed
When everyone got the money mange
Lots of money and dearer homes
But still we heard the regular groans

Lies, deceit, promises, threats
Murder, muggings, rape and jet sets
Gays, lesbians, heteros and AIDS
Rent boys mostly under age

Please God, the nineties
We are as one
Race hatred, really gone
And even more, no dreaded bomb

The ozone layer we will restore
No fears of poverty or war
Let's make it, please, so very clean
So 2000's England can be peacefully green.

Habit

Naked, dressed, flying pests
Nasty substance, painful chest
Kids and dealers, dangerous game
Needles, tablets, razor lines
But really I am not to blame
Heroin, cocaine, black and a leb
Dirty needles, sick in bed
One-time hearts and now it's E
Should the dealers be left free
Hit them hard, lock them away
So all our kids are free to play
The past is yours
The future theirs
So open up the doors for care

Full Circle

We are toddlers now and going to primary
Growing fast, new school, it's secondary
Grown some more, now local college
Pass exams, set off for uni
Time for fun, a little joy
Catch someone's eye and they respond
Walk in the park, time for a cuddle
Weekend home to meet the folk
Ring time, now we are at the jeweller's
Now it's time to meet the vicar
Wedding bells and then the feast
Into bed for a night of bliss
Pregnant now, time for a family
Again it starts, back to the primary

My Furry Friend

Apricot with a touch of white
I should have been Ginger
What's in a name? They tried them all
Then Jan came up with Tinker
Walking proud around my path
Sending other fur a-flying
Head held high, my mane, all fluffy,
Jump on my stand, please let me in
I give that look, you know the one
Please turn the window catch
Miaow! Miaow! Am inside now
Heading for the kitchen sink
Turn on the tap for me to drink
On the floor, a pot of prawns
I know I'm spoilt, I'm such a toughie.
Creeping up the stairs to bed,
My eyes all bright, I pad my pinkie
Cuddling up to Janet's arm
I know I will not come to harm
Curl up and then lie on my back
To sleep now, my lovely Tinker

River

I'm small, I swim towards the sea
Following the flow so easily
The time to grow is fraught with danger
Although I feel no anger
I feed until I am big and strong
Then the day I need to breed
I turn and swim the way I came
Back upstream against the current
I need to jump the waterfalls
I lash my tail and wave my fins
Then I conquer all my trials
Back to the shallow water
I brush the gravel and lay my eggs
Then born, my babies swim to sea.

Cats

We have a cat, a lovely chap
He also has a sister
They chase, then jump, *ouch*, fight and spit
Then settle down on my settee
I do not hear a whisper
Birds landing on their table
It's full of seed for them to feed
We could begin a fable
Sparrow, finch and robin
Blackbird, thrush and tit
Both cats, Dobbin and Bobbin
Locked inside, no way out
About to have a fit!

Better Times

The trees are green and full of blossom
Bushes, hedgerows full of berries
Farmers' crops grow strong and healthy
Insects thrive, the worms are fat
Bees work hard to make more honey
Eggs have hatched and birds are feeding
Field mice climbing up the wheat
The profits in the pub are growing
Horses rubbing on the fence
Shopping trolley filled to the top
House prices rising very high
And new cars in all the drives
Sit back now and watch the telly
Well-fed now with a big fat belly

Passed Away

Time has no time
Light no light
Darkness no dark
Space is endless
Sunshine no brightness
Moonlight so dull
Rain no wetness
Snow no whiteness
Ice will not slide
Warmth has left us
Earth is so damp
Life has gone.

Love And Hate

Why do we preach we have a land of love
When really we have a land of terror?
We have a faith, it's what each believes
But then each faith wants to reign supreme
We then get angry and kill each other
God's Son, Jesus, grew up to be a Jew
He would never think about shooting you
He didn't preach the word of hatred
Nor teach the world the reign of terror
It's time to teach our faiths mean friendship
And we really can all live together
It must be better than war and hate
Get rid of bombs, the tanks and planes
Have happy bodies, not dead remains

This For Fun

The fox's hunted by the hound
He's hunted till he goes to ground
And then dug out to the huntsman's shout
Ripped until his body's shredded
Is this what hunting's all about?
The pheasant reared then shot
Another sport or barbaric lot
They save the birds from the mouth of Reynard
Then hunt and shoot them like our dear old fox

Winter Feed

The branches bend in gale-force wind
Branches bare, the leaves all gone
Birds and squirrels are easily seen
Feathers spread, the fur blows back
Watching on the muddy ground
The neighbour's big black cat
A ginger tom crouches closely by
Not sure where to pounce
A barking dog on the bridleway
Chasing a big brown rat
Both cats turn, their fur all spiked
Birds fly off, the squirrel jumps
The dog is called to heel
The ginger tom he chases off
Big black cat feeds off the big brown rat.

A Life In The Day

Speeding cars and motorbikes
Charging on the motorway
Do they care? I think not
High on blood rush they want more
Pushing towards that deathly door
Traffic cops take up the chase
Safely speed to catch up
Switching to the blues and twos
Both chaser and pursued
Go faster, faster, faster
Way down the road a car is crawling
The driver filled with drink
Speeding drivers close the gap
The drunken driver takes a nap
Car swerves across the lanes
Speeding driver braking hard
Twisted metal, blood and cuts
They now have found that deathly door

Spring

Springtime shines with young new flowers
The blossom sweet and grass dark green
Blackbird song, his babies born
Swallows end their journey far
Sunny days, long bright nights
Flies and spiders feed with delight.

Think On

Don't give in to the prejudice, bullying, abuse or racism
Stand up straight and take control
Learn, forget the world owes you a living
Go to college, age is not a barrier to knowledge
Be respectful, be not vain or egotistical
Love yourself as you would love others
Teach the world to be people-friendly.

Beauty

There is such beauty in your face
The beauty you say does not show
Like flowers in the early spring
For me, your beauty always grows
Like roses bloom no man can buy
It makes my heart so want to cry
Your skin's so smooth
With eyes bright blue
Oh yes, I am so in love with you.

ADEGOKE A ADEDAMOLA

He hails from Ibadan, Oyo State. He attended Ibadan Grammar School, Bishop Phillip Academy, St Andrew's College of Education and he holds a BSc(Ed) Agriculture from Ahmadu Bello University, Zaria.

A handsome and God-fearing gentleman who has practically combined creativity and intellectualism with politics; he has written many poems published in different anthologies with Forward Press Ltd, United Kingdom, and still has several poems waiting to be published. His work is focused on the intrinsic values in men's lives, the most abstract parts of the nature of humanity that make life more meaningful and rewarding such as love, fame, money, nature, beauty etc.

Adedamola says . . .
'Writing poems comes as a result of the need to inform others of thoughts that flow within as directed by the unguarded inspirational impetus of circumstances, situations and conditions in which I find myself at a point in time. Thus my mode of writing is simple, straight but firm in thought to send the intended messages across without any ambiguity whatsoever, as poetry itself is an expression of feeling as it comes from the source without dilution. I do not have a specific interest as my mind dictates the tune of my writing as an expression of thoughts centred on motivations, inspiration and appreciation of feelings, while my recurrent themes tend toward romance and important events as they are unfolding in my environment.

Create Your World

The power of creation
Lies in men's minds
The power to create your world
Lies in your hands
The power to live your world
Lies in your self
The world of your own is the
World you build by yourself
It may be the world of politics
The world of entertainment
The world of music or
The world of inventions
The world of the known
And the unknown
The world of uncertainty
The world that is full of despairs
The fear of building your world can
Lock you up in a world you do not cherish
Those that build a successful world
Always have a tale to tell
For there is no glory without story
And there is no gain without pain
For the world of success is not an easy world
It is the world of hard work and
Commitment, faithfulness and dedication
To the cause of your action
Rise, create a world of your own and
Be a successful man in your generation

Fame

Popularity is not by accident
It is a process of decisions
And a product of actions
Your popularity can be negative or positive
Those that are cherished by others are
Bundles of achievement in their own world
Popularity is not accidental
But a creation of action
Ignited by thoughts
Though it can be spontaneous
It comes with glory and honour
From fellow men
Who have discovered uniqueness
In your personality and have found
An uncommon ability in your activity
A famous man is a man of purpose
Those that set a goal and
Achieve their objectives
Those that know the essence
Of life and the value of nature
Those that understand the complexity
Of Man and sincerity of nature
Those that make hay while the sun shines
Those that invest in the lives of others which
Makes them live longer in
The memories of their subjects
A famous man is always a man of mission.

Money

Here you come as a visitor
Visiting those that need your attention
When you come around you
Make a difference
When you are not around
Nobody can take a decision
You breathe life into lives of many
You make living a pleasure
And full of comfort
You transform scarcity
To super abundance
You are a dependable servant
That can solve many problems
Your ability to unite and divide
People is unquestionable
You can erect a community or pull
The same down at your own discretion
Your power of changing or
Transforming lives is undeniable
You can make a ragged man
A rich man within a second
Your power to defeat poverty
Is never challenged
You can solve a million
Problems within a moment
No wonder many are seeking
For you round the corners
Many have gone to places to seek
Your attention because you are
The most valuable thing everybody
Is looking for but you are
Where you are till the end of time

The approach and manner of
Seeking makes the difference
Most especially
When you choose those
You wish to visit
Then the more you quest
For money, the less
You see it coming around
Money, when you come around
And stay around, life is more fulfilling
Because you are the only desirable thing
That answereth all things
Ironically, there was life before
Money was in existence

Promise

When we said it we meant it
To do the things we said we would not do
And the things we said we would do
Promise, a strong word that gives
Hope and assurance
In times of despair
Promise, a word of comfort
In times of need
Promise, a soothing word
During a great expectation
Promise, a balm to those
That need its comfort
Promise, a tiny string that holds our
Belief and faith together; promise
When fulfilled it is quite rewarding
When it fails it is very distressing
Never promise what you cannot fulfil
Because it is a great debt
You owe to mankind
Promise, there is no word
Like you in time of need
But a failed promise
Can be so disappointing
Because it is a dashed hope
With lost expectation
But a fulfilled promise
Can be so refreshing.

Wonders Of Nature

Nature is naturally opening up
Things are coming back to where they belong
The world of nature that is full of wonders
That beauty that was made undiluted
The essence that purifies the lives of mankind
The wonders that suffer men's imaginations
And worries the hearts of men without solutions

Is it the fresh water that is flowing from the rock
That means nobody knows its starting point?
Or the sky that is turning black and white
Based on timing and seasoning?
Think of the ants that build their hills
Where it is calming
Or the lilies that are open and release
Their fragrance without informing
The natural mountains that are positioning themselves
In artistic scenery, so huge and so high
You keep on wondering
What is holding them from falling.

What about the valleys that spread
Deep and down to nothing?
Or the rivers that flow in the direction they choose
The big and small animals
That give birth without attention
Naturally reproducing their kind without assistance
Young plants germinating with support from nature
An open vast land that bestows its beauty
To fresh green plants that grow lovely and beautiful

The everlasting wonders of nature that surpass understanding
The splendours of the world that beat imaginations
The perceptions that are incomparable
Nature that is naturally opening to nature
The amazing, marvellous dexterities
To which no one has an answer
But we've all agreed to call it 'Nature'
Since it is eternally full of wonders

Dear Mother

Whenever I remember
What you are to me
I always appreciate
The work of God
You are the one that sheltered me
You are the one that nursed me to grow
You are the one that catered for me
You met my needs when I needed it most
Is it the care or love you shower on me?
Is it the affection that runs naturally
From you to me?
All the things you've done for me
Can't be exhausted here in one day
For whenever I reflect on them
I appreciate you more
You are the golden mother among the rest
Mama, your care has made me grow
Mama, your protection and provision
Have made me understand your worth
The values, norms and traditions
That money can't purchase
These you gave me freely
Without compulsion
I love you daily with all my heart
You are the inestimable jewel
That money can't buy
I cherish you always, my dear Mom
You are the dearest of all mothers
In the whole wide world
May you live long to reap
The fruit of your labour
For I will surely repay if time permits

A Letter To Jack

Dear Jack, my precious dog
This piece is for you, my little dog
To appreciate your loyalty
Commitment and faithfulness
To me and my house all the time
I remember when you used to be a puppy
Beautiful, robust, cuddly and friendly

I carried you around like a baby
With a name that has a meaning
Now you have grown and still
Look cute and chubby
With commendable neatness and smartness
That is quite impressive
Dear Jack, you are just a dependable companion
And a good escort that loves his people

Only you cannot speak out your good intentions
But by instinct I do get your message
Whenever you bark or growl, I know what you want
When I speak, you obey my instructions
With all devotion and affection
You are a fearless guard without a bullet
A good security guard that defends his subject

Dear Jack, I am always dazzled by
Your intelligence, wisdom and dexterity
Most especially, when you do amazing things
That surprise my neighbours and make them wonder
If you were a man whether you would have been a genius
And possibly won a Nobel Prize in your generation
My dog, what a wonderful creation you are among creatures

Heartbeat

Give me a thousand diamond stones, it can never
Be enough to compromise my inestimable love for you.
You are like a gem from a very deep blue sea.
You are my heartbeat in terms of love.
All the love inside me has been asleep for so long,
But a glittering gem has woken it up.
The gem that sparkles love into my life
And turns me around for good.
Honey, you are my heartbeat.
There is nothing I can use to compare your love for me,
That is why I have decided to make you my golden love,
Gently placed on a golden fleece
And carefully guided with golden eyes.
Never forget your love for me,
Let it glitter all day long,
Let it be blissful all year round,
For the sake of something we all cherish,
The love we have jointly built together.
Remember, the start can never be like the end
For the end is always sweeter than the beginning.
Sweetheart, I have made up my mind to love you forever,
That's exactly what I will love to do.
My promise for you is an infinite one,
To love you and care for you all my life
With love and affection that knows no bounds.
Honey, if I could buy your love every day
I would pay a supreme price for the love you give
Because you are my heartbeat in terms of love.
Remember, if you take away your love
The heartbeat may stop.

Valentine's Day

An emotionally laden day that parades
Itself among the little lovers of the world
Sharing the same emotional conviction within them.
A day lovers come together in unity,
United by love and enjoy the moment.
Lovers come together to enjoy the day.
A special day set aside for *love* -
A day that comes but once, for little lovers
To test their love and express how much
And what they mean to each other's lives.
A day that emotions and feelings flow like rivers
With different kinds of gifts that speak of love
With words of affection that come with it,
To launch their feelings of love on each other's hearts.
Gentle, sweet words of love that soothe the heart
And set the mind ablaze with excitement.
Little love of no importance grows great on lovers' day
When more light is shed on it,
It then radiates and expands on lovers' minds
For the benefits of love dwell right here with us,
Therefore, let us love one another,
For the reason we live, is the reason of love.

SUSAN VANGO

I live in Isleworth and have four children, three of whom are now grown up and flown the nest. I first started writing at primary school where I would create picture story cliffhangers and sell them to my peers. Unfortunately demand outstripped production, but it did enable me to buy something from the tuck shop in those days.

I first started writing poetry in 1990 when I met a fellow poet and work from those days is quite 'dark' and forms an ongoing dialogue between us. I'm now semi-retired, having worked in further education for many years and since last year have begun to write again and have been fortunate enough to have several of my poems accepted for publication within different anthologies such as 'Immortal Verse', 'Body And Soul', 'The Creative Touch', 'Natural Beauty', 'My Small World', 'The Art Of Poetry', 'Poems For Mum' and 'To Paint A Picture'.

My poetry is not of the conventional 'nightingale, sunset, love and beauty genre', but rather asks questions of humanity, the world we live in and beyond, whilst retaining humour and sometimes becoming political. I'm strongly influenced by everyday events and people surrounding me. Writing, for me, is a form of therapeutic exorcism of my heart and soul.

The following collection of poems is a mixture from the 1990s and more recent work, some already published and some unpublished.

How I Write

The pen jumps into my hand
And the words tumble onto the page
Emptying my head
Exterminating my rage.

No time to stop and think
Of perfect metre and rhyme
Everything stands still
Unaware of natural time.

Oblivious to all
Until we're really through
Servant to your call
I only feel your pull.

There And Back

Wheels touching tarmac, skidding down the way
Lush green reinstated of my green and pleasant land.
Whizzing down the M4 entranced with drizzle, cold and grey
Breathe in the fumes and the odour of my town.

Kick open the door, pull in the bags;
Smell the perfume like a stranger, disorientated and tired.
See the wallpaper peeling, a house made up of rags.
Remember anew the moments, the family I sired.

A vision of our lifetimes to sustain us through the days
Obtained through the familiar tried and tested
Delighting in the grind; obliterating the pain.
My home, your home, full of senses, sameness
A comfortable belonging, built on drifting sand.

Letting Go

She didn't want to go, my mum
Fought it all the way
Her body riddled with disease
But knew it was a cloak anyway.

Sat there all day long, praying silently
Not that she would come back to me
But that He'd release her from the pain
And do so gently.

Finally she laid back on the bed
And fitted uncontrollably
I knew then I had to clear my head
And let her soul soar free.

Close your eyes and travel with me
Far above the stars
Close your eyes and you can see
What waits for us afar.

Close your eyes, see the kaleidoscope
On the other side
Hold my hand, I'll go with you
I'll abide with you awhile.

Feel the love unconditional
What beauty is for real
Know you're going now for good
My resolve turned to steel.

I know it was a forbidden glimpse
Of what mortals shouldn't see
I know I promised I wouldn't cry
But it was easier for me, you see.

Going Over

Words spoken in earnest
Definitions of my mind
Going back to timelessness
To seek and to find.

Leaving life behind
And all that we know
Seeking out new meaning
To test and try and probe.

Finding you beside me
Wrapped in satin gown
Knowing that you'd be here
Comprehending now your frown.

Out-Of-Body Experience

Popped out my head
Left my body behind
Flying way up in the sky
Like an eagle soaring high.

Hovering and sauntering
Over my domain
High up in the atmosphere
Where it doesn't rain.

Seeing things you told me of
Things I can't explain.
No words or visions relevant
Then it starts to fade.

Snapshot From My Mind

Put down the mop and bucket
Cast the broom aside
It's a well-earned break I'm taking
To rest my weary hide.

I wonder if you notice 'Chairman of the Pride'
That from this high plush office
Where you secretly smoke and hide
There's a great scene of beauty just outside.

Gaze through the window sipping my tea
See the willow and the stream, pure tranquillity.
I don't know where this scene is, disorientated and high
But when I need it back again, it's there in my mind's eye.

'Oh, sorry Sir, I thought you'd left'
I quip appeasingly
You bang the door to quit quickly
Looking right through me.

For My Children

Stop and take my hand, my love
And let me walk with you.
Let me carry your despair
And truly understand.

Stop and take my hand, my love
And stay with me awhile
I will ask for nothing more
Only for a smile.

Stop and take my heart, my love
Keep it fragile as a flower
And when I'm long and gone from you
Rekindle as a form of power.

All Grown Up

Words shot in motion
Icons drenched in wine
Your bloody face still dripping
Through the tunnel of my mind.

Shirt torn and drenched
Resignation on your face
What could I do or say?
Realisation of your race.

Burying my anger
But crying deep inside
Wanting to take the fight for you
But acknowledging your pride.

Watching the sun come out
Pebbles drying from the rain
Standing like an old oak tree
My son - now a man.

My Baby

Pulled from the dank darkness
Of my body, legs astride
I looked at your cramped-up face
And felt a well of pride.

Your hair was bloody on your head
A fist clenched against the world
I knew in that one moment
This was love and beauty intertwined.

Neighbourhood Plague

Ring at the bell, impatient, knocking wild
It's old nosy parker with a cuppa in her hand.
'I'm not one to gossip but them across the way
Music blaring all night long, like a percussion band!'

Telephone shrieking. It's Beth on the line
'Had a letter of complaint re the litter in my drive.
Been round to nosy parker to find out what's the matter
Wasn't her, it's them across the way.
She heard them having a natter.'

Knock at the door. It's the RSPCA
'Your hound's not walked, your cat's not spayed
We're taking them away.'
Round to nosy parker, confrontation's on its way.

See old nosy parker - eyes blank - nose pressed against the pane
Quietly contemplating who's next for the frame.
Wasn't her, she knows nought, never one to complain.
Another day, another year and there she goes all alone
Poor old nosy parker shuffling down the lane.

Quick Lunch Break

I sense your rudeness
Sitting on my bench
Swigging from your Diamond White
Absconding all pretence.

I heard you bring up wind
Your unwashed body close to mine
I heard you talk your rubbish
Seeking that still to find.

I watched you stumble
Shredding paper bed on your way
Scratching your unshaven stubble
Wondering about today.

Animal

You pluck it from progenitor
And put it in a cage
You circle like a panther
To exercise your rage
You spit at it
You claw at it
You violate its home
And in moments of benevolence
You proffer up a bone
You purr at it
You play with it
To alleviate your grief
And then you roar and pounce again
And shake it between your teeth
You go back out to hunt again
And return in awful rage
Your eyes are green and wild again
You forgot to safeguard the cage!

Gone Too Soon

Smell of Golden Virginia,
bicycle clips in place;
being lifted up so high
where nothing really matters.

Walking in the pouring rain
in shiny new red wellingtons.
Holding your big paw so tightly,
splashing in the puddles,
secure and safe and happy.

Playing on my fifth birthday,
riding upon your broad back,
seeing my best friend take her turn
experiencing a new taste so sour.

Three days later you are gone
and I watch the door all day.
And when I ask about it
Mum says nothing, or occasionally,
'Look, he's up there. See the big star.'

Fifty years have flown by
and the void you left is great,
but sometimes on a warm evening
I stare up at that star
and I'm safe, secure and happy
cos, Daddy, I know where you are.

Sandy

Oh Sandy
Victim of humanity's harshness
Opening doors just to slam shut
Never to go first
Nose pressing against cold glass.

Standing pregnant and wide
Waiting for the seat
Never to be delivered
At your feet.

Oh Sandy
Expectations built on social niceties
Always to be disappointed
By that which is selfish man
Forever waiting patiently
For the right time, place and man.

Josie McGregor

I remember all those years ago
When you wanted to play
I belonged to the gang majority
And it was you we had to slay.

Hearing the bell chime
Following you sly
Predator of the lonely
Making you want to die.

You weren't like the others
That was your crime
The reason we had to pull your hair
And torment you all the time.

I know I have to take the blame
But I wonder about the others.
Do you surface in their dreams too?
Do they hang their heads in shame?

Or is memory selective
As we hold our babes in arms?
Following a correct directive
Creating false protective balm.

Optical Illusion

Sitting in the chair
Trying to read the letter
Feel your breath upon my face
'Now is this any better?'

Shooting lights into my orbs
Violating my space
'Or is it better without?'
Powerless in my place.

'You say you want the tinted lens?
Your vision's a gradual deterioration.
That's two hundred and ten right now
And a possible future operation.'

Poetry Per Se

Simile or metaphor?
Iambic or trochaic?
Anapaestic or dactylic?
Who wants to read it?

The poet who writes?
The intellectual elite?
Let's go back to rhyme
And reclaim the seat.

Confined to the Masters
Lost to the masses
Creativity withheld to
The lads and the lasses.

Specific or commentary?
Third person or first?
Interior or slant?
Let's say it as we speak it
And make sure we mean it!

MARIANA ZAVATI

Mariana Zavati was born in Romania and studied languages and literature. She is an MSc graduate in Philology. She is the author of poetry, short stories and translations published in Romania, UK, USA, Canada, Germany, Israel and Yugoslavia. The *Daily Mail* has published her first novel, *Miss Mariana in Black and White* in 2006. She has been presented with the Bronze Medal in the North American Open Poetry Competition 1998, The American Romanian Academy Award for Poetry 2001 and The *Ionel Jianu* Award for Arts 2001. She regularly contributes to Romanian literary publications.

Mariana lives in Norfolk.

Julia May's Cats

There were long corridors of snow
Outside the icicled windows with
The crack of so many years
No one even tempted to mend
The secretive flat with the cats
Roaming the beds and the chairs
In great need of repair and the lights
So dim one couldn't well see to sew
Or repair clothes . . . the frozen nights
With shushed tales of wild beasts
Who might have ruled or tried
To settle old scores in the land
Plans and visions of journeys
Into remote places one sees in dreams
The old cats were purring life
The even older woman was trying
To catch a glimpse of the young cats
Knitting fantastic chases and hunts
Her eyes were no friends who
Could grasp the gist of those letters
Arriving from dazzling places
One never feels welcome but where
People continue to live with the tide
The old man and the even older woman
Were alone with the old and young cats
In the flat near the station where . . .

Limestone

The girl stumbled
On a stone born of lime
It was clearly stated
In her chemistry book
She was so bored
At the turn of the day
Dragging across the room
With paintings in oil
Bought by Julia May
From artists who lived
In a provincial town
Cool darkness remote
From the afternoon rain
Blue paper at the windows
To nurse the heat of the day
The summer was gathering
Speed dripping in sweat
Like a ballroom dancer
Unable to figure the steps
Too drunk by the heat
The rotor of thoughts
Drenched by tunes settled
From mechanical devices
Her head was digging the cushion
Her hand was resting by her body
The chemistry book at her feet

Summertime

Our summer visit was in the mountains
The desert was coughing with dust
The sun was biting and cracking the light
The afternoon was preparing to die
Above the Music Mountain lizards
And cacti were fighting for spaces
Like caged grasshoppers were singing
The sky was burning an oven display
The spaces of stone were all around
Much stone and sand to spare and no water
Displays of turquoise beads were on view
And sand pictures from legends
About some people who vanished
And left their thoughts behind
Some in stone, some under the soil
Red from the iron ore to touch
And feel their wandering souls
At Little Bighorn and beyond

Time

The Black Forest clock,
My young husband
Bought last fall,
Was flapping its wings
The rain was coughing
The willows were dead
The wood was drifting
Unknown destinations
Tormented birds
Insects in heaps
To feast from a potted disease
The ginger tomcat left alone
To mark the angular garden
Which was breathing dust
When my young husband
Bought it from the clockmaker
In a remote Norfolk village
Time, an extended condition,
To tell over shouting grasses,
Of lovers' hide-and-seek
Places where young people meet
The Black Forest clock
Stopped its wooden wings
On the bookcase at home

Searching

She played hide-and-seek
In secret chambers
Where tapestries
Long in waiting rooms
Woven in needlepoint
Slow-moving afternoons
Scented evenings to seek
And escape from love thoughts
Ravenous oak to hide
Dying swans on dying waters
Dry feelings from crossed voices
Her perched anguish
Was clawing his heart
The day was diseased
Indifferent, it was about to drown
Sudden lapses and changes
Vouchers exchanged hands
In the courtyard with a bricked path
Under the linden trees about to bloom
Claiming immunity from expectations
About immaterial love born
In the format she knew
Silence was to follow the sound
They blended in metal
Armorial costumes

Little Town

In the South East,
There is a little town
Little now, but extending
Quite forgotten
Some might say
With antique bus shelters
And posters with
The Union Jack
And a bandstand
In the Queen Mother's garden
In the sunlight
On a Sunday afternoon
Echoed sounds
From the music reflected
On the stone walls
Of the Norman church
From the middle of the town
In the luminous High Street
The best of Britain
Displays grow from the depths
Of the cobbled streets
That border houses of brick

Instructions For Children

Do this, do that!
Open the window
And close the door
Put the washing in the washing machine
When it's done, hang it on the line
Must not forget
To say 'please' from time to time
Place the dishes neatly
In the dishwasher
And don't forget the salt
It's time to fill the container
Most of all, don't forget
The saucepan on the hob
Wipe your shoes on the mat
Must not forget
To say 'please' from time to time
Do this, do that!

I Had To Do

Run for the bus
Rush
Rush
Rush
Forgot the key in the lock
And the milk at the door
Run down the alley
Rush
Rush
Rush
Nearly fell over the ginger cat from next door
And the dustbins
Still unemptied of garbage
You were there standing
A blueprint waiting
For the bus to go
To the city or to the coast
Who are you
A prisoner of timetables?

No

I do not want to listen
To the same stories about
Exciting travels to South America
With slides to match
I'd much prefer not to listen
To your voice giving me advice
About various points of view
Regarding the anatomy of our home
I don't have the slightest curiosity
To exist as your sounding board
I am not the least bit interested
To laugh at your jokes every night
No way am I going to wish
To discuss about transatlantic flights
I am simply not able to share
The excitement of your replies every day
Strange as it may seem I do not wish
To hear the clock every morning
There's nothing I'd like less than
To sort out the knives
I regret I do not want to drink
From your love cup every night
I refuse to answer
The phone, the email or answer the door

Persistence

Thick rope betwcen death and night
Fragile dreams of drought and water
Holy memory of choking
Coffins displayed in algebraic forms
Crosses shrieking on a window

You make me sleepwalk
Amongst the pews
My palms made nests for growing bats
You made my cells vainly stir
And bagatelles overcome
Wires, needles and drips
Shafts of ghosts in absolute
Subtle crafts and graphs
Your definition of the quick
And the dead, vainly
In acrobats' costumes

Your rose looked down
From its waterless vase
Exiled on your bridge of sighs
The absolute, another thought
Unable to define
What happened next!

In The Andes

Wrapped tight
In icy linen, starched
On the glass mountain

Wrapped tight and
Left to soak
In alabaster breath

Wrapped tight with
Snow on airy hands
The smell of lead

Wrapped tight
A gasping mouth
To suck the earth

Wrapped tight
No vault, no breeze,
No flowers made of lead

Wrapped tight
In fluid sleep
A scream turned into stone

Wrapped tight, a silver toy
Hurried from place
By the noon wind

Julia May

Julia May was stuck between
The four walls of a dream
About humming pens on paper
And water dripping by the well
In the old courtyard

Julia May was able to feel
Houses of iron
And houses of brick
Over the park, peppered with
Electric lamps and bird droppings

Julia May was able to see
Shadows of people awake
In her dream town with heavy doors
Over the park, on the first floor
Of a townhouse, on her now island

Elisa's Dream

The shutters opened with a jerk
The day gripped the street, the whispering
Senior cherry tree; Elisa was now the night
She was waiting to part from the trees
Her soul was gaining ground with the light
Abruptly fading and gone; it was too late
There was no cancellation; an unwanted flight
Elisa was waiting to meet Ion beyond
The orchard, the beehives and the cherry trees
The peach tree that Ion did not want to plant
Still there, by the window, the lead sky
Sour storms, of blue considerations
Very soon no one needed to worry that afternoon
The shutters closed with a jerk: Elisa was gone . . .

GILLIAN MUIR

I live happily in Leyton, East London. I was born in Crouch End and educated at Hornsey High School for Girls. I then taught in secondary schools in London and Nigeria for over 25 years.

Independently, I raised two daughters who 'light tomorrow with today'.

From the age of 15, I immersed myself in the poetry of T S Eliot, Wole Soyinka, D H Lawrence, Chaucer and a host of others. My many influences include Audrey Jancovich, Pete Doherty, Zeb Achonu, Jay Muir, George Mackay-Brown, Bob Marley, Bob Dylan, Dylan Thomas, Beverley Knight, Terri Walker, Linton Kwesi-Johnson and Angie Stone.

Recently, I came back from Westray, an often remote island.

I enjoy the immediacy of urban poetry and art exhibitions, poetry evenings, local gigs, the Hackney Empire, Stratford Theatre Royal, trips with Waltham Forest's Photographic Club and places where I can feed my spirit.

My husband Cecil is a tremendous support who encouraged me to sniff around the old houses of his mother's homeland to complete my anthology 'des res'. He is my audience and appraiser. I thank him.

Fealy Ha Risen

Parly-a-ment
Parly a
Parlay voo
Inky pinky parlay voo

Crows glide over from Fribo Woods to
where Fealy Ha was black with boys
in those days
going down to where Doubtful stood
on the curve
on the brae
jostling and mingling
in long breeks
so they say.
Where were the girls?
Fealy Ha became their parliament
large-lummed,
headed by bearded men and elders
dark with dirt and pipe reek.
It was black with boys in those days.

After the artist had digitally pipped
and watercoloured the uninhabitable,
when the ewes had pushed their nosy noses
against the dandelioned doorways
and calves had joined in, doggie-curious,
the roof gave way and the men stacked in half-dozens
the flagstones
ready to flog to the south.

Fealy, wreck of memories of chatter
and testosterone and male initiation of tribal mores
and pubescent boys grown to men
was left awhile until the market was ripe.

In magnificence
and sheer defiance she held up her gables
before the handing over
from useless to full.
The calves were breeding now and the ewes rammed too.
Time had overtaken the picture the artist drew.

The Tribute To A Ruin

Past the chatter and incessant murmur of children
in the buzz of the evening sounds
of midges flying against bulbs of oil and paraffin
of hammer on heel of boot unsewn
against clod of cow and reek of coal from sooty lums
of banging of dough on wooden table
by arms strong with milking
past all this and a pile of memories
my mother-in-law and I drove by Netherhouse.
We went slowly for fear of running over the ghost
of a child playing in the mud
poking the corpse of a rabbit run down by a cart.
We slipped slowly past the walls of the blackened inside
of the once busy smithy. I saw nothing:
she saw the man bent over his work, his mind on a thousand jobs.
She saw all that in the dim of a circle of light.
And she smelt the red-iron heat.
A tattered curtain of flowered design marked the poor
as it wafted, shy by the door.
There was no jug or tin or any old thing
on the window sill.
Only I imagined the life within.
My mother-in-law knew more. She had her memory
about every house doing the same.
If the mother washed her hands in the butt outside,
so washed a hundred others, too.
If the grandfather moved slowly from bed to hearth,
then her grandad did, too, and every old wife did spin.
'We were all the same then.'
Kerb-gawpers, we never came out of the car for the mud was guttery
and the settlement inclined on a hill
overlooking Gairy.
We never knew who was about with ten others and a gun.
Nothing escaped us.
Upwards against the blue sky shaped the crow's feet patterns
                              of the roofs.

North Tuan 2003

The tall pencil-black chimney of Ramsay
showed no excitement
on October 15th
but gazed across the road
cow-eyed and unblinking
when the roof fell in on North Tuan

collapsed then sprang an ugly, grey surround
tufted opening
apertured
and orificed hag-woman
knickerless and rude.

Gone were the lines of sloping stonemason
            booted, bearded male grace
those were down then
defiled by the gape.
In one night the flagstones met each other
            fought
            and multiplied.

Across the way, Greenwall turned her back
            in despair
and cattle entered her loins
to suckle her mineral-dripped stones.
From her straight-back walls
black rectangles of window holes
looked out to ghosts of homes.
She had retired silently.

Highly sloped, majestic and new
South Tuan overlooked the overlooked.
'Out with the old!' she hooted
clashed as a voice in a man
from a wall harled without ancestry
and ignoring heritage.

'Out with the old!
Bring power lines to every door
and pink fur wall-linings.
Make paths meet each hard front door
and decorate your lums
with dishes metallic shining!'

North Tuan stood proud for decades
harboured at the edge, for generations.
For decades, felt the clank of pail of
milk
left to curdle and whey
or the sillocks
twined
to shrivel and shine in their iridescence
of rainbow sheens
or water
fetched from the well
stored tightly indoors
when the sea lapped up the shore
leaving her gift of rotten cat wee
stinking kelp
and foundlings from Armada wrecks
of china dolls
stashed away under thorn bedsteads
and wooden poles
and rope twisted by Indian men
on her mauve flagstone floor.

She echoed the tinny noise
to the top of the steam-riddled walls
in which the pig circled her nest
and rooted for memories of scraps.
Pig in the hole
cock at the door
and kitlings in every barn.
All manner of generations sheltered
from the storm

and North Tuan
filtered the squeals of children
and the grunts of the pig
from the hush-an'-stop-that-greetin'
muffled, stifled, sobbing, grieving
of the
bereaved and stricken,
as TB and drownings stealthed away
the brightness of life
and dimmed the fire in the hearth.

Springs returned again and again
and the daughter of the house
ruffled amongst the dog roses
which earmarked the ditch,
ran errands for her father
to wave to the passing steamer
and dreamed
of a different service in life
above the fog of baccy buying and fish
bait tying
in stewardessing.
Titanic massing.

She turned, saw Tuan
left, married, and dutifully returned
to the cold hearth
to the cold of Northern Isles
to wire-brush her parents',
sister's and brother's headstone,
tied her headscarf, churched her knees,
gathered the roses' roots
and planted them in her husband's way.

On the barbed wire fence
which prohibits her descendants from
feeling her walls
and window spaces
from stroking the pig hole
North Tuan has her private funeral.
Black ribbons of plastic
shredded and escaped from man-stacked bales
want to ride on Westray's winds.
Spitting barbs spite the flags
to half-mast them
and commemorate a falling down.

Netherhouse

A carnivore crow flapped her wings and unsettled a century of dust.
She skulked her eyes then stayed put
with talons gripped
on the remains of a chimney.
Her sleek black back snubbed the newly growing box
                                        of a house at Gairy.
At Netherhouse, the derelict abandoned village,
and her new-found platform,
there was an ungrowing and a caving-in of yet another roof.

She-crow perched, waited patiently
and tapped the column of lum stones,
where beneath, in the vaulted chamber next to sparrows' skeletons
white like porcelain and chicken snaps,
fragile and frail,
ready to morph into dust of ages and 'Time Team' forensics,
lay corpses of rabbits side by side, mass-graved
and matted on the floor.

From inside the room and gloriously scented wafting
into her beak-nose
came essence of vermin.
Run out and bred fully the old mixie bunnies came to die.
Eyes like those of mackerel slabbed on marble
at fish-mongering outlets, had long since melted.
Long thighs were in running position, foetid and unfurry.
She-crow had found her trove, was guarding it
and planning rabbit retrieval.

Once or twice a car wound by.
Sometimes a farmer wending his way to dinner
or a house-viewer passed by,
eyes ahead,
never looking to lums.

She-crow was about her business without interruption.
Bunnies were blindly entering her pit.
She smelt the warm fur and earth-stained flesh
as it moved in the massing of tics and fleas.
At the door she would catch the meek behind the nettles
and the blue star-shaped flowers swamped in greenery
which paved the way for pink campion.

The Day After The Cree Indians Danced In Westray

Today on a rotary washing line
I spied fish drying.
They were cuithes, grey in colour
and unappetising to all but the fish-feeders and the gulls.

At the next house, I saw not a flag roof:
that was down, but a leaning lum
and knew the incomers had come and were about to stretch
a line of juice as my husband called the light.

In the wild, the seawater across from Nebrille
looked fresh and good to drink;
reminded me of the razor advertisements
and surfers in the roar
of the clashing, crashing turquoise blues of the ocean.
A bore hole's soon to be dug and drilled.

There were nasturtiums at Tirlot,
cheeky Tom Thumbs dotting orange and red on the old
stone dyke
and the wall was smiling in her new pinafore.
The keel, thick, bulbous and solid wanted to
cannonball the chicken-wire boundary,
wanted to join in the sun,
roll by the rolling dogs,
and stop in the tracks of the old wife homemaker
as she pinned out her garments on her own swing-about line.

Overnight Cottage

Time ago my ears were assaulted by sirens;
now they open willingly to birdsong
in the darkest hour before dawn
at 4am.

A tortured chorus of wind seeks direction
in the black distance
bumping into grass mounds and humps
on the mouths of disused quarries.
Like a cat
it slinks and crouches
and replaces the mechanical hum of
factory din
in my life before.

I am trapped cosily and nervously
in a dark place,
with flagstones underfoot
dented and scratched by testaments to
ancestral lives.
Flagstones like tombstones have fallen
and hide graves of bones.
The black outside stares through nine-inch
squares of window.
She blinks and flashes back
horror movie-men with grins.
Gnarled fingers tap as the willow wands
stroke ancient quarried stones
then argue with the wind.
There are no urban shutters to defend me:
I close my eyes.

JOHN GREEN

I started writing poetry about twenty-five years ago when in hospital for several months, but most of my work has been written in the last five years.

My main themes are war, love and spiritualism, with music, films and personal experiences providing most of my ideas.

Why Mother?

Mother, why does Father scream each night,
Is it ghosts that give him such a fright,
Why can't he run like other men,
What brings on coughing fits again.

Mother, why does Father not talk of war,
What happened to make him feel so sore.
Why does he stare straight through me,
His eyes are fixed, what do they see.

Mother, why does Father always curse the Hun,
When opening the trunk containing mask and gun.
Why can't he be like all the others,
Painful memories bring on the shudders.

Mother, why does Father always take it out on you,
Beating your body black and blue.
Why must he drink so much gin,
Is fighting for your country such a sin.

Mother, why does Father mutter 'mustard gas',
Can he picture it drifting to engulf a mass.
Why does he march just once a year,
A cold November Sunday brings back the fear.

Only Fools Fight

Only fools fight, putting their lives on the line,
Volunteers, brainwashed into following the recruiting sergeant.
Led down the garden path to where the grass is greener,
This is the last time many of them will smell fresh flowers.

Only idiots accept the King's shilling,
Jolly Jack Tar sailing the seven seas.
Sickness ebbs and flows through tightened stomachs,
U-Boat captains wait patiently below to press the button.

Only imbeciles climb into flimsy planes,
Taking to the high arena for pit bull dog fights.
Cumulus carnage, a twenty-minute teenage massacre,
Victors notch another kill, losers spiral to an early grave.

Only clowns would sign up for this crazy show,
When the balloons go up it's time to perform.
The ringmaster cracks his whip and off they charge,
Into the lion's den, the silly smiles soon wiped away.

Only conscripts have no choice to make,
Called up to do their bit for King and country.
Cannon fodder for desperate generals and politicians,
The real truth hurts, not only fools fight.

Crying Days

It's one of those crying days today,
God only knows what sets them off.
This little grave in front of me,
A one-way ticket to the tissue factory.

How can a grown man cry so much?
Where do those tears well up, deep inside.
What triggers off this steady stream,
Into a gushing torrent, looking for eyelid escape routes?

A boy who will never kick a ball with me,
Nor sit and read, nor even have a dream come true.
I cannot bear it, each and every hour,
Letting go from time to time to ease the pain.

No rubber-duck, bath-time splashes and bubbling laughter,
Or sing-along videos in the dead of night.
Outfits and toys, bottles and bibs,
All crossed off the shopping list.

A nativity play goes on, a little angel short,
At sports day, one less egg and spoon required.
No bicycle to master, a tour de farce,
The Enigma code of ties and shoelaces never to be cracked.

A gentle lullaby only I can hear,
One candle, but no cake or party games to play.
Schooldays and homework never an option,
No cap and gown, nor any rites of passage.

So every desperate now and then,
I curl up into a ball in the corner of a room.
Howling like a banshee, my own primal scream,
A dozen dangerous emotions thrown into the melting pot.

I sit alone in a time-capsule nursery,
Wallpaper, hopes and dreams torn and tattered.
Toy soldiers waiting for orders that will never come,
This is my never never land.

Chalk And Cheese

Let me tell you a story about a couple of boys,
enjoyed playing soldiers, guns were their toys.
They did not use names, just chalk and cheese,
their schools were different, so were the fees.

A time came to fight, over in France,
they didn't know that they hadn't a chance.
Training came first, learning the game,
they thought it a laugh, who should they blame.

Oh my dear Sandhurst, what can you supply,
sending boys out, to lead men to die?
Eighteen years of being a child,
then sent to their deaths, you must be wild.

When the end came, and the last shot was fired,
nations were sick, even the generals were tired.
Millions had died, so many still missing,
mothers cried, loved ones kept wishing.

Look at the battlefield, men on their knees,
two boys lie dead, chalk and cheese.
War is not fussy, nor is it fun,
and money and background can't stop a gun.

Give Us Our Daily

Give us our daily bread,
a hungry world needs to be fed.
Millions starve, we wine and dine.
They are condemned, we feel fine.

Give us our daily meat,
animal slaughter, quite a feat.
Just to put upon a plate,
please change tack, it's not too late.

Give us our daily loaves and fishes,
empty bowls or fancy dishes.
Lake of wine, mountain of butter,
what a waste, I hear you utter.

Give us our daily milk,
Many lie on straw, a few on silk.
Some live on nerves, others hope,
we try to help, but cannot cope.

Give us our daily food and drink,
the mood is black, we are on the brink.
Wild flowers growing in the ground,
mushroom cloud, atomic sound.

Give us our daily blood,
sea of red, tidal flood.
Defence talks failed, a bitter blow,
ice age approaches, crimson snow.

We Are All Lost (Labyrinth Life)

A starting and an ending point, the only sure things in life,
All the rest is labyrinth, a life of twists and turns.
Disappointment or joy around every corner,
So many dead ends, little sign of hope.

Blind leading the blind, we are all lost,
Playing follow the leader down the garden path.
The Lone Ranger is in charge of crowd control,
Not even the sun, nor the stars can guide us out of here.

Beasts of burden, with a heavy load,
Pushed and pulled, beaten and flogged.
Slaves, branded, inspected, sold at the marketplace,
Tangible assets, with a street value of diminished returns.

Papering over the cracks, trying to stop the rot,
A crying baby probably knows its fate.
Strike up the band, its shake, rattle and roll time,
Dancing on the ceiling, swinging from the light.

A famished polar bear is knocking on my door,
My igloo is melting, and my canoe is up the creek.
The compass points are spinning as I run across the ice,
Heading in ever-decreasing circles.
I manage my life on goodwill, but I am running out of credit,
No structure to my molecules, they do their own thing.
Only the lost boys around to ask for directions,
To keep me on the straight and narrow.

Forgotten where I was heading for, what a fool,
On a hopeless, clueless treasure hunt.
The tracker dogs are all off with colds,
And my once faithful homing pigeon now plays away.

Chocolate Soldier Hero

When your chocolate soldier hero melts in the heat,
find another sweet boy's shoulder to cry on.
And your icy snowman starts to thaw,
pray for another cold spell.

I showed you all the signs.

When your long-distance jogger runs out of puff,
don't come sprinting back to me.
And your rugby hunk no longer tries,
don't throw me a pass.

You ignored all my warnings.

When your muscle man turns to flab,
stare at the dumb-belle in the mirror.
And your tattooed heart-throb gets the needle,
stitching you up in familiar patterns.

You got what you deserved.

When your gorilla gets put behind bars,
find out his visiting hours.
And your heavyweight champ hits the canvas,
another one fails to beat the count.

I never pulled any punches.

When your senses come back to you,
see me in my true colours.
And your beefcakes are no longer on the menu,
I might be waiting.

Pavlov's Dog

You treat me just like Pavlov's dog,
Ringing the bell to see my reaction.
Yet here sits a lone wolf,
With a reflex of freedom.

Call me atavistic,
Get me jumping through the hoops.
Then back into the doghouse,
A no pain, no gain way of life.

Pushed and shoved into trap one,
She keeps me on the rails.
Off we go as the hare is running,
Boxed in, nothing but a sandstorm kickback.

A hare's breath moment later,
The other dogs are home and hosed.
But Pavlov's dog becomes a lame duck,
Even the tortoise plods on past.

Put me in Skinner's box, a guinea pig,
Deserted by the rats, learning to push the lever down.
Food for thought, my just rewards,
The lab coats note it in their little books.

When spring arrived, she said take a hike,
Plague dog, unleashed into the great unknown.
But now the leaves and icy rains are falling,
Pavlov's dog is treading water in the quicksand.

Huntsville, A Monster's Ball

Take the last train to Huntsville,
A warm reception at the station.
One-way ticket, no way back,
Private, en-suite room, without a view.

It was murder trying to get a ticket,
To this evening's Monster's Ball.
Lonely souls in this lone-star state,
Where lethal cocktails are all the rage.

Smoking old sparky is no longer the host,
Seething and smouldering, unplugged, he sulks in the corner.
Replaced by a syringed serial killer,
Full of venom and menace to make you thrash around.

Pardon me Governor, for I am an innocent man,
Is there any compassion under that ten-gallon hat?
Fill your cowboy boats with remorse,
When my healthy lungs collapse.

Up on Thirteenth Street, it's unlucky for some,
The crowd walk to 'the Walls' and campaign for or against.
Vigil veterans opposite the tape, they know the score,
Silence falls, heads go down, another life taken.

No hunters or trappers here, but always a kill,
Capital punishment, vote-catching flavour of the day.
In Captain Joe Cemetery see the white crosses,
Another freshly dug hole, a telltale sign.

Comets And Baby Turtles

A plumb line to measure my very depths of despair,
To fathom out the oceans of utter uselessness.
Drowning in a vat of sorrow is mildly amusing,
Anger fermenting, tuns of barrelled bitterness.

A chain reaction, set off in my unstable head of steam,
I dare not broach the subject with anyone.
This jewel in the crown is crumbling to dust,
Pinpricked ego, humiliation ringing in my ears.

A storm cloud, bulging with a sack full of acid rain,
Dropping its load on unsuspecting innocents.
Quenching their thirsts, cups running over,
Burning desires, etched lines on furrowed brows.

A seafront of shifting sands and fortunes,
Shabby pier, like me well past its prime.
Windows rattle, boats stretch and sigh,
Seagulls shout salty warnings, distress flares fill the sky.

A crack of dawn, another day to try again,
To piece together fragments of my shattered nerves.
Talk of the town is of my rejuvenation,
Back from the brink in the nick of time.

A gallery displays my offerings, and the critics arrive,
Feeding frenzy, not all sharks live in the sea.
No destination for my escape mapped out yet,
Gutter press trying to attract my short attention span.

A comet appears, and I know it must be a sign,
We all drop off the radar and return from time to time.
I need to travel far and near, out of sight, and out of mind,
Baby turtles and I break out, and rush towards the sea.

Uncomfortably Numb

Here lies this English Patient,
Loosened stuff shirt, stiff upper lip.
Nerve ends tingling, but not with excitement,
No more feelings, numb, uncomfortably numb.

These feet will never slide into another pair of boots,
Or walk where the ocean flirts with the sandy beach.
How many miles have they carried me,
My sturdy ships of the night?

The white coat gets his hammer out,
Then whacks and prods with no flicker of emotion.
Charting a timetable of steady decline,
A downward spiral into the abyss.

Suffer in silence, or shout the whole place down,
I am hurting, leave me to think dark thoughts alone.
A shaded room, a drink or two, or more,
Memories of better times drift in and out.

To dream, of slowly rising from the bed,
Crippled, walking-stick man, unsteady and unsure.
Fighting demons, slaying dragons, jumping hurdles,
Immobilised, paralysed, rigid, wooden block.

Very still life, painting a pathetic picture,
No poetry, just grinding to a standstill.
Give up the ghost, fall upon my sword,
Winding down, an appointment to meet my maker.

Walking the plank, with a millstone dragging,
I learn to be calm, but no sense nor sensibility.
Too many snakes, not enough ladders along the way,
The final reel has rolled, the show is over.

Information

We hope you have enjoyed reading this book - and that you will continue to enjoy it in the coming years.

If you are interested in becoming a Spotlight Poet then drop us a line, or give us a call, and we'll send you a free information pack.

Alternatively, if you would like to order further copies of this book or any of our other titles, then please give us a call or log onto our website at www.forwardpress.co.uk.

Spotlight Poets Information
Remus House
Coltsfoot Drive
Peterborough
PE2 9JX
(01733) 898101